SO, STRANGER

SO, STRANGER

poems by

Topaz Winters

Button Publishing Inc.

Minneapolis

2022

◆

Published by Button Poetry / Exploding Pinecone Press
Minneapolis, MN 55403 | http://www.buttonpoetry.com

◆

Cover design: Talisa Almonte
ISBN 978-1-63834-024-9
26 25 24 23 22   1 2 3 4 5

Contents

SO, STRANGER

Departure Time

Through noise-cancelling headphones the plane
engine growls audibly as a hallelujah chorus.
For the last week I have been finishing
the things left undone. Now as I rise I regret
double-checking that I packed my passport
& toothbrush instead of collecting proof
of having loved. Proof of having once
been from somewhere, belonged to something
that knew me whole & still chose me back.
But now, on a layover at a glass airport that
shimmers like mania, I bathe in suds of noise
at Subway, evidence of the living. I nibble on
a white chocolate-raspberry cookie, its familiar
staleness a bridge stretching ten thousand
miles back to what I've left behind. I text
each of my best friends, ask them to send me
their favourite memories of us. Even now
I am so full of hubris & hope. The ones who
should be asleep are the ones who text back
first, & what is this ache but a method of
survival. When I get up to use the toilet
before I board my final flight, I hear a woman
sobbing in the next stall over. I can't decide
whether to knock on her door, say something,
anything. There is a god in this but I don't know
if I have already returned him for store credit.
Instead I stay in my own stall until I hear
a conspicuous flush to my right. Outside,
the woman stands in front of the mirror
with red eyes, smooths out her hair, avoids
my gaze. In my mouth my tongue feels strange
& heavy. I want to forgive something & she's
the closest thing in earshot. She walks

out the door & a minute later so do I,
in time to see her laughing next to a man &
taking a suitcase from a small & eager child.
There has to be a word for the kind of
loneliness shared by two, a loneliness
big enough to rechristen itself as lineage.
I'm grateful when they walk off in
the opposite direction of my terminal.
Like a game of hide & seek with both of us
waiting to be found—I can't help but think
that together on the same plane the weight
of her distance & mine could bring down
the whole sky.

I.

Ars Poetica I: Every Day the Same Story About Immigrants

How their tongues curl around
that bitterness called language.

How they wake in a futureless
country & shrink-wrap it.

Swallow it to possess it. I know
this story by heart, by which

I mean what kind of daughter
am I if I don't: my grandparents

with their plane tickets to
a place too big for its maps.

The accents they scrubbed like
caked lard from their tongues—

& the way they tell it now, this
being less an act of violence,

more one of devotion. My father
in his teenage years thinking

America America America—
& the way he tells it now, this

being less an act of obsession,
more one of communion.

& here, now, there's me sitting
at the dinner table, eating roti

prata, chana masala, listening
to this story instead of living it.

A white girl comments, offhand,
how surprised she was to find

I have no accent, & I have to bite
my tongue to keep from snapping

*it's an American accent. That's
not the same thing.* Even now

my rage is the spitting image
of my father's, but unlike him

I have no right to it. Every day
of his life he has fought for this

brilliant stricken language, this
country as a brand of fire he

wields proudly, generously. I sit
with my bloodright in three

different time zones. I listen
to my grandparents flare Tamil

jokes across the table, accents
arrowed & twisting around

what they've left behind. I know
this story by heart, geometric

in the face of shapelessness.
One moment my grandmother,

working beyond recognition.
Boarding a flight for the first time.

Learning English because how
else will America read her love

letters. The next she reaches
across the table to pass me the

dish of aloo, whispering a Tamil
joke I only half understand

& love anyway. A prayer I
can wear out loud, a wound I

can salt into keeping: this is
how we tell our stories, hold

our promises. Become again as
our languages grow animal, silent,

as we echo in the etch of bigger
births, as we keep living anyway.

I Found a New World Across the Sea

& in this world i am the good wolf in this
world i am the good witch i am
never fed & never hungry

i am gentle in this world i am the
shelter not the reason to go searching
for it in this world when i worry too much
it is cute instead of pathological

in this world the first boy i kiss does
not run the moment he sees
me for what i really am

in this world the first girl i kiss
i do not call her god

i do not want so loud i morph into cannibal
when i starve it is inaudible i leave my body alive

in this world i am never so lonely that
i laugh just to have something
to wrap my hands around

in this world i am no longer a list of
unasked questions & the answer to each
is no longer the word blasphemy in
this world when the parts of me that
are not made of water beg for mercy

i spare them

So, Stranger

if your body is a country, open your mouth.

Swallow down the drought & the distance.
Fold your limbs & follow them back

to the light blinking against a Michigan
afternoon where some blue-eyed
girl you love is loving someone else.

Her good heart irrepressible, strung
of apple blossom, false cartography.
Sun eating sky until that sky

stops beating. Stranger, you disappoint

everything you touch. It's
a special skill of yours—pollution,
another word for progress.

Once she kissed you & it felt like
picking up exactly where you left off.

Now you're ravaged into silhouettes,
her touch stings like quicklime,
you yawned without thinking & suddenly
all this distance. God you're tired,

& god you want to be wanted, & god
fits perfectly in the space between her mouth

& the American dream.

So, stranger, what invented you as emptiness?
How much of your love is a training exercise?

Truth: you are, you exists, you immigrant soldier
never fell for anything in reach. Truth:

when you tire of your rivers, daylight will always
outsing her to your country, will always
beat her to your doorstep, will be
the first to witness you undressing from

your failed miracle of a body, bones clicking
away from skin, tendons all
loosening, unwinding. Truth:

she human. She exit.
She scraped knee, efficient even in wounding.

This time the apple trees bloom year-round,
not just when it's convenient.

The poem closes around you like a map,
like a bodysuit. She breathes against you.
You search for a zip.

War Story With My Father

Any dream, as long as it begins
     with treacherous. With mercy
          borne back & restless from the
    fingertips inward. If I'm lying
through my teeth, at least I still
     have the long way home. If this
          is where my father ends, at least
    I still have his hands for ransom.
I say *you are every reason I cannot*
     blink anymore & he says you can't
          blame me for all this gasoline. It's
    enough for the knife & the
tongue. After him there are no
     ways to make dusk small again.
          No method to serenade grief
    soft enough for the streets to
swallow. You can't undo glory.
     You can't force a home to
          unwind & fix itself. My mother
    tells me that my father only yells
because he is afraid. Finally,
     something we have in common.
          I see the hurt in his eyes when
    I flinch as he tries to hug me &
I want to say *it's not your fault* but
     all that comes out is *I swear there*
          was a time when I didn't starve in
this language. Dislocation in car
window & my father spins
     creation on the rooftops. All
          my little achings with no sleep
    to dampen. I've only ever prayed
to avoid rescue. My father grins

out a haemorrhage, blood behind
            his eyes all black & narrow, a
        night extraordinary with all its
heart. I say *these are dangerous*
        times to be a daughter. He says
                enough with the metaphors,
        you're making your mother sad.
I speak in vowels without oxygen
        to spark a murder. Fury is just
                as human as fear & every girl
        I've ever brought home tells me
I have my father's smile. I'm
        beginning to understand why,
                even in sleep, all hospital car parks
        remain full of hope: home is not
my father's hands but the light
        they reflect when burning.

Birkshire Lane

the first life is overripe apples / a ruinous melting / eyes closed / radio static / sweetness scarring the back of my throat // my mother braids my hair in the morning before school / & gives me the tools to survive: / *this is how you boil water* / *this is how you give someone the finger* / *these are the only things you will ever need to know* // as a child i recall my stomach must cave before all else / when asked where i'm from i say / my great-grandmother died a month before i was born / & since then no one's eaten the apple pie on the kitchen table // often i am nothing but a plastic fork / nothing but a metal knife // my mother drives me home & asks, her voice a landscape marred by sorrow, / what i learned in school today / her grief is the first soft thing i will ever touch // some places we live twist us to unbelievers / but every day this house grants me a new ghost / a new pair of lips to cry for / a death chastised into birth / a kindness without ulterior motive // on the table, the apple pie aches to taste a tongue // my mother & i stand in the driveway holding mirrors that don't exist // even now, in the frame of beginning, i am not a god / but i am a girl, at least // a girl / a time to exhale / a pot of boiling water / a reincarnation, or at least revelation // i turn down the radio / i miss what i never knew / i fall asleep with cinnamon stuck in my mouth // where my mother has forgotten how to cry / & it smells of evening / all afternoon

II

Ars Poetica II: Season Finale of the American Dream

We don't say *how are you* anymore,

just *you doing okay?* It's a good enough
substitute. The answers are equally

obvious: *fine, thank you,* & *no, of course
I'm not doing okay.* No one is doing okay.

The only ones doing okay are the ones who
don't need to ask. At the grocery store,

the Black cashier searches my eyes before
giving back my change. Tells me to take

care. I have never seen this man in my
life, & still I know he will stay up tonight

wondering if I got home safe. These days
every letter I write to my girlfriend ends

not with *I love you,* but with *I am so glad
we are both alive.* I don't say goodbye

to people anymore. I am saving my
goodbyes for something that feels more

& more inevitable. I want to be ready
when it comes for me. In some lights

these consonants look foreign, torn, but I
will not allow them any name less than

manifesto. Make no mistake: this is not
a story about hatred, it is a story about

fury. You can do a lot to our language but
you can't make those two words mean

the same thing. The woman who lives next
door to me is a Khmer Rouge survivor. I

was with her when she learned that a man
who brags about sexual assault is now

our president. It is the first time I have
ever seen her angry, & now I know how

she survived. Now I know how we will
all survive. Make no mistake: this is not

a story about fear, it is a story about
what happens when we grow tired of

being afraid. I walk down the street &
the existence of my body is a room

made entirely out of knives. Yesterday
my sister told me she was going out with

her friends & I tried to say *have fun* but
what came out was *are you sure you want*

to wear a skirt that short? You cut your
teeth on every new language we burn in

& we sing more radiant, more jagged still.
You think everyone here is full of fear.

Make no mistake: this is not a story about
fullness, it is a story about starvation.

We are so hungry we are bloody.
So hungry we are frantic. So hungry

we may never eat again.

Relapse

America says *I am disappointed in you* & I say
join the damn club.

I pick up the phone mostly because it's raining,
& my father says *how come you never
call me anymore* & I say *how come you never
take your meds,*

which we both know is avoiding the question,
but at least the next morning my mother
tells me he has taken his meds.

America says *I expected better of you* & I say
great, that makes one of us.

My father & I don't fight over the phone,
which means we don't talk over the phone.
Apparently the parenting books say

it's supposed to get better when the kid
moves out, & I'm nothing if not a rule-breaker.

My father says *you can be anything you want,
but you can't expect to live off it.*
America says *you can be anything you want,*

but you can't expect to live.

My father is an immigrant, which means he
walked into America's mouth, not out of it.

I'm a daughter, which means every drop
of rain on my head is saliva from
an animal only as hungry as it is hopeful.

& why else am I here, really, except
to keep my father from relapse.
To keep his body awake

from three oceans away—America
says *you are full of wasted potential*
& I say *at least I take my meds every day.*

My father says *I miss you, call me back*
& I say *not every sickness is hereditary,*
but more than you might think.

I'm told it was raining when I was born but
when I try to imagine it I can only see teeth
—an animal groaning in its sleep,

jaws wet & closed. Unswallowed pills.
The September sky weak with distance.

I was born in America. I'll remember it

into reality. I imagine I was born perfectly
healthy. I imagine my father told me
that he loved me, & for once in my life,

I imagine I believed him.

Dear Monsoon

To name you girl & delight in being destroyed.
Is this romance?

Water is too good at forgetting. What a mess
it makes of us. Still we call it gentle, don't we

—belong less to ourselves
& more to the salt that birthed us.

You, girl, monsoon. A sky craven
with geese headed somewhere better.

I too have been beached on the shore
of every promise I've broken.

On my worst days they fit just so
in my cupped palms.

They say I have my mother's palms,
my father's sadness.

My mother says most of the sky is invisible to us.
My father says he still dreams of flight.

Dear monsoon: to name you girl.
To spend the day drenched & unthreatened—

what a use of a body is this.
What do I want? A jacket that fits,

not to keep you away but to keep you safe.
Come inside, then, & kiss me like you mean it.

Or, if you won't, at least leave me like you mean it.
Leave the windows open when you do.

Is this romance or memory?
Has my father forgiven me yet for drowning?

You, girl, wasteful. The drought came so suddenly.
What can I do now with my palms?

Lover of Light

In the backseat of the Uber I could be
anyone I want & for some reason I still choose
to be other. The driver asks if I am Spanish
& I say *no, Asian*. All the mistakes
I might yet survive glinting around my
neck, & I am thinking of my grandmother,
combing my hair at seven years old,
telling me about Lakshmi & her thousand
candles. Thinking of my father's namesake,
lover of Lakshmi, lover of light. The Uber
driver says *but your name doesn't sound
Asian* & I say *my family is from India*.
I was eleven when I realised I didn't know
how to pronounce the place where my
mother was born. I was fifteen when
I chopped all my hair off & walked into
her home with my neck bare, an evolution or
a treason. Too old then for my grandmother
to comb it for me, too proud to believe
in gods with more than two hands. The Uber
driver says *so you're not Asian then,
you're Indian* & I am thinking of all
the horizons whose backs I broke to get here,
every name I faked to make my way to this
white woman & her GPS on the dashboard
saying fourteen minutes until we reach
home. She says *I'm really into yoga.
I want to go to India & get a guru—do you
have any recommendations?* There is a story
where Lakshmi & her husband find
their way out of the woods after fourteen
years, following the lights in the windows
as though no candle ever marked a grave.

But they make it. It's a happy ending. I
think about my mother whose name means
light, my father whose name means *lover
of light.* I think about my grandmother
who did not cry when I cut off my hair, or
at least not in front of me. Would I trust
a god who promised me relief of this huge
& gorgeous debt? Would I become a
different other, shed my blood like snuffing
out a candle? The GPS says eleven
minutes. I am a coward or maybe I am just
tired of questions I don't know the answer to.
Instead of responding I point to the growing
sunset outside the car window, take
a photograph on my phone. The auto-flash
is on & when I look, the photo is white
& overcome, its sky drowning
in man-made light.

Where Are You Really From?

A country where no one ever leaves.
      A salvation in unlikely constancies,
             my people, you crouch, you memorise
      the sun beaming high in rafters, trace
it down, you swallow it in your throats.
      I see you & your voices, the blurred
             glow when you speak. I see your sleep
      orphaned by arson & afterbirth. My
ear's to the concrete like only she
      knows which suicides are real. You
             & I, my people, where we come from
      we lick our teeth vacant, exhume sound
to crown our gums. This is how it goes
      when we gift our bodies to a season.
             Our shame outliving our shadows, all
      the little madnesses that make us in
the heat. I'm from anything but quiet,
      from long past midnight, from death
             by déjà vu, mispronounced as memory.
      Where am I from? A flicked switch. A
bad habit flushed into air. The rain so
      in awe of our knuckles, how many
             colours they can bruise in. Each time
      we leave our country the years drag us
back home, paint us in sweat, what we
      left behind. My people, I think of you,
             I think of that involuntary gravity, taut
      between the streetlights & the tilting.
I leave & I lose my grip on liquid.
      The night opens its jaws, births me
             into lightning, I'm from a country
      where no one leaves until the dry
season hits. We scatter then, like

raindrops broken under pressure. We
    know each other in the world only
  by our knuckles: tender & raw, skin
split wide open, telling a story of
  everywhere & nowhere at once.

III

Ars Poetica III: This Must Be the Place

of all the languages to scream in   my favourite is the
brown body   raw sugar skin   buckling washboard rough
        threaded in a needle's dark dark eye
    at the temple my grandmother speaks   wild animal
speaks   fire & rolling seascape   third
resurrection shredded   stripped hungry for six years after
        her husband's death   saltwater caressing
her lungs to execution you   could unkill a woman
    with the length of fabric in her sari   brown
body with stomach to ground   with birth as disaster
    with cow-god in the sky frowning down   on
our one-night joy   strangled into poetry
    pregnant with ghee & honey   have we too lived
in the walls of an atlas   have we inherited our parents'
shame   our children's joy like oxygen   or
fingers mid-snap   meanwhile my grandmother spins
a peace offering in blood   scrapes dirt from skin skin
from dirt chants   क्या तुम मुझे प्यार करती हो
    क्या अब तुम मुझे प्यार करते हो   meanwhile brown
body   bottom of ocean   brown body says नमस्ते means
    hello bone marrow   means everything it says
    means revolving door synonym   for leaving
    brown body sees everything hears   nothing
    if the poem is the sister of the map   my
grandmother   shines at the temple
    dances to death   says everything i have i
gave to my language   & now she won't even let me
    in out of the heat

That Summer I Wrote the Same Poem Over & Over
for JS

It always came in flashes, pristine as a rebroken
bone. The walk to the ends of the world or at least

ours, fever of monsoon season whittling through
our throats. Every night the same park, the same

dark—what else was there to write about, that
first summer I learned to be beautiful as mutiny.

Watch can be verb or noun, omen or gift. Eyes
everywhere & never enough time to carry dusk

to its finish line. That summer we were almost
angels. We pushed back the dry season with our

bare hands, came home each night drenched in
each other's sweat. In that park I learned how to

be someone's greatest fear, by which I mean I
learned what belongs to me. I learned that pawn

shops make you sad the way funeral homes make
most people sad. Learned that every night after

you saw me, you went home & sat on your bed in
the moonlight & plucked the feathers off your

back before you went to sleep. I only thought
about the word *miracle* with your palm in mine.

The world moving but not heavy. From behind,
each passing auntie could've been your mother's

best friend. Call that a love language, breaking
apart at a familiar silhouette on the pavement.

Playlists set to *private* on Spotify. I didn't want
to die, I just wanted to love you. You bribed your

brother with convenience store cigarettes, watched
him lie to your parents' faces for you. I couldn't

have inherited a more stunning betrayal. That
summer I wrote the same poem over & over, &

I've never been a better poet. There was a time we
had gorged ourselves on promises: Rome, or New

York, or *one day, when things are different.* Now
all there was to promise was a walk tomorrow

night. Your laughter teasing open the dark, so
sweet. No one saw us unless we saw us first. At

each blink, another uncle on a well-timed grocery
store run, family friend on the way home from

work. It wasn't about us so much as the spectres
we imagined into words. Smart girl—do you

know your parents are so proud of you, even
now. Do you know summer has gods of its own.

Do you know which of your mouths wants me.
Do you know you can write the same poem a

million times but you can only wake up once
from a dream. In the right hands, a kiss can

be a crime scene, & I've never loved anything
without something to hide. Feathers in the

garbage can, excuses in the cigarette box,
stop me if you've heard this one before—

Ship

Imagine writing a father without writing a drowning.
For the longest time I recoiled when he touched me,

my body weighed down by that cureless mercy
of looking away. My glasses are smudged with

the things we've agreed never to say. The bottom
of my purse is scarred with his cologne. This

part hurts to write, which is probably why I don't.
Never mind. Let's reduce it to facts. In the photos

I am his spitting image, not the other way around.
My mother says *you argue because you are so*

alike, & I am too young to be this lonely around
the person who loves me most. Maybe that is

the truest gift he will ever give me. Half the answers
to the questions he asks me are *it's better if you don't*

know. Maybe that is the truest gift I will ever give
him. We're screaming at each other over the phone

again. This must be an heirloom too, right, how I
hang up & recoil when my lover touches me next?

My mother says *when you don't pick up his calls*
you are grieving for a thing you still have & I guess

what I'm trying to say is no one ever told me there
was another way to grieve. How am I to forgive

myself for always being the one to leave first? How
am I to forgive him for loving me in a language

I've never had the lung capacity to learn? We
are always in the process of destroying each other.

I have only ever seen him cry over me, have never
once seen him flinch & look away. When I swallow

the sea he wakes up gasping & I am sure of nothing
except that I'm sorry, I'm sorry, I'm still sorry.

OCD Litany

In the city of pears I walked everywhere instead
of taking the bus. When my father called the first
time I picked up. The second time I was asleep,
or pretending to be, & the third time I opened
my eyes wide & bit the nose off my phone &
listened close until the ringing, by blood loss or
shock, drowned itself to quiet. I summoned my
wounds in the dancing night, & when I awoke
the scabs christened my bed like dew. At home
it was the Year of the Rat but here it was just
the end of January. I still filled my throat with
rice to celebrate, less asking to be spared & more
asking to be known. Like any good girl I was
invisible, but like any good girl men still
catcalled me on the street, so like any good girl
I turned & gave them the finger, then transformed
into thousands of live moths batting against their
cheeks. I took two doses of Prozac & in my
filthy stomach that too became myth. I went
to the laundromat to pick up my spine but it
wasn't ready yet, so I sat on the washing
machine & waited, dwarfed by my own shadow.
The years moved past so loudly it was almost
like they were trying to impress. Every building
in the city turned conscience, exhale, & I mean,
it was raining but it seemed only logical to walk.
Night saw that I was alone & offered me its legs.
I turned to no one & said look at me dance & it
was January forever, or at least for a long long
time. Nine months. Maybe more. There in
the rain my father kept calling & I was moored
in a pirouette between the sidewalk cracks of
sickness, weighed down by my air-dried spine

& ballet shoes, my desperate bid for immortality.
What kind of world did I live in then, with
moths blocking out light in the search for it.
That's what he said to me, over voicemail—
you know you can't call it a superstition
anymore if it comes true even once.

Tame

Brown girl meaning body starving with
thirst. Brown girl says open mouth or
window. Says death is how you make
grace. Brown girl says I'm here. Its horror
good & fevered. Guilty as a sole survivor.
Brown girl forgets everything it's ever
loved, calls that growing up, calls that life
sentence. Very polite is brown girl. Speaks
only when spoken to. Brown girl lives
sober. What other choice does it have.
Brown girl sits in the house before the house.
Bloodline pooling in its lungs. Reticent.
Brown girl not all holy no matter what
it wants you to think. Scraping out the
corners of its scream. Unshut unsplitting.
Head down for a potty-trained language.
Brown girl naked on the bed meaning scared
to be beautiful out loud. Brown girl is
its own act of violence. Says I can hear
the salt on my skin. I can be animal too.
Just watch. Brown girl says will it hurt
very much writing my own pronoun. Who
cares. Watch. I have hurt enough to be real.
I will tear my country from between my
thighs before I ever give you the chance.

IV

Ars Poetica IV: Still Life as Lover Unarmed

Poetry, you said, is a room full of mirrors,
none of them glass.

I can go with that story. I can undress as well
as any crime scene. I'm good at softness, the noun.
At ruin, the verb that enables it.

Here I am & here I am again.
I'm a tremor of trees whipped into sun.

I'm so in love with you I want to live.
I'm so in love with you it forms the beginning
of every circle.

So maybe that's the only truth.
Voltage hissing in the air, all warm.
Even the quiet has teeth.

Of course I changed my mind,
came back to haunt you. Of course
you could teach me any dirty word
& I'd call it praying.

Poetry, you said, is the monstrosity
of being wanted.

I can go with that story. Find me
like sucking poison out of a wound.

I am better than I was & still I disappeared. & still
you didn't die in that hospital.

I'm thinking about you, which means
I'm thinking about leaving.
Which means I'm thinking about bodies
& their gruesome politics.

Dimples. Seizures. Daytime.
What we inherit. What

we owe.

Poem in Which I Am Too Uncomfortable to Talk About Race, So I Talk About Baseball Instead

To uncage the arms, reach toward home
& miss the base. Ball unraveled into
stitches. Each hand a designated hitter.
Here comes contusion I may never
escape: a white boy I used to call
my friend texts me to commiserate
about election results, immigration
policies, the third mosque in his town
the victim of another mass shooting
Every pulse point I own spells *ground
out, second base, how could you begin
to understand?* We might've had a rain
check, but my eyes are dry already.
Outside the window a ball curls through
the air, quick as hair freed from helmet.
Slow as wrists freed from shackles.
The next day, white supremacists
riot in the city where he's playing
the next leg of his baseball tournament
& he is the one who calls to ask if I'm
okay, not the other way around. Look
at us, covering all our bases & yet so
afraid. That night he posts the hashtag
#AllLivesMatter right after a tweet
congratulating his team on winning
the game & a retweet of a cat with
its head stuck in a watermelon. I
want to ask him not to call me again
but how could I listen to his heart
roll in the dust across phone lines,
each word in my throat waving its
awed & welcome arms? Instead I say

congratulations, I say *is the next*
game being livestreamed, I'll try to
catch it after work, the ball raising
him up even as he bats me out
of left field. He asks if I'm feeling
all right. It's so easy to know what
he will never know. I tell him I think
I'm coming down with something
& hang up the phone first. In some
other place, winding & slow,
an umpire yells *safe.* Yes. Safe.
We are all so full of that sound.

जन्मभूमि (Ten-Week Confessional)

Just look at me,
dreaming in sea-language again.

/

I can start without the jasmine in
my mouth. Build a temple to want,
a Navaratri I can count on one hand.

/

So all I remember of my ancestry
is what fits on the back of a postcard.
It was a long time ago. Can you
blame me for my childhood betrayals,
for closing my eyes a split second
too soon? I am the furthest
thing from finished. Spin three times
in front of the altar. Keep spinning

/

I'm tired of begging for forgiveness.
Give me joy. A bindi on my forehead.
Nine planets. My mother's
hand in mine.

/

Maybe I'm a decade past whatever country
I should have packed in my carry-on,
& maybe regret means nothing
without an exit wound. Hindi

melts on my tongue like sugar on hot idli,
my parents reaching North to South,
midday daughter half in shadow,
half in light.

/

If I could have anything I wanted
I'd still be here, shoeless in
the same room, repeating
the same questions.

/

Most days the ghosts wear my saris
better than I do. Pause my blood. Here's
a curfew. Here's a bell.

/

Parlour trick: watch me disappear &
reappear as hunger. Or better,
watch me never reappear again.
They teach us the gods prize girls
who take up the least amount of space
but still I can't help wanting to be found.

/

I'm counting the bangles around my wrists.
I'm watching a priest give
an elephant god a bath of milk.
My selves are tired. They guard
a hope with henna on its feet.

/

Everything I created
never made it across the sea. I didn't
even get to watch it all drown.

Ghost Field, 1999

In my monsoon dream of hunger
the first thirteen years were a swallow
down the back of my throat. At each
dinner my family set out an extra
plate for our unsaid sickness, &
maybe I have always been running,
but never toward medicine. At
thirteen I was terrified of ending in
the same place as I began. I wanted
the only violence I created to remain
soundless, rooted. To make sure
the house I left my love in really did
burn to the ground. I wasn't making
that up, like I do with so much else.
The bathroom mirror is repulsed by
itself, my birthright a bottle of pills
& newly formed devastation. As
they say, a knife in the hand is worth
two in the throat. It's just a folktale
but only in the dry months. Does
this sadness mean I owe the world
nothing or everything? Morning rain
is the worst for remembering & my
want for death is my most marketable
skill. This isn't goodbye: I'm drunk
& I love you. I'm determined to know
your legal name & I love you. Heritage,
meaning scripture, meaning cuffed
& lucky in rain-shattered light. You
were always interested in saving
my life, or what was left of it anyway.
Instead we ran, instead I was every
verb except the one that would

put an end to all that looking back.
You said *you always have an alibi
in me* & for once in my glory of
a life I believed you. The unmooring
of the wrists is absolutely out of
the question: I've learned all I need
to know about stillness. In these bird
bones, there is no noise anymore
that couldn't pass for music.

Before

i imagine memory began
with my father in
his childhood dancing

the chessboard of his
own intelligence & anger
to hear him tell it now

you'd think he knew
all along of the country
gleaming in wait at

the end of a tunnel
made of decades today
my father speaks

of america the way
the impossible seems
inevitable the moment

it has happened but
what he will not tell
you is the first time

he left he didn't bring
his passport to the airport
with him he had never

realised he needed proof
of his country to leave
it behind & meanwhile

my father's father refused

to watch him go instead
he tossed in sleep futile &

floundering in bedsheets
& blackened pride &
meanwhile my father

turned his back on the
border of everywhere &
began to sculpt a myth

that named itself orphan
in his adopted language
& meanwhile my father's

fury turned common as
a mango or more rare &
meanwhile each decade

between my father & his
homeland lapped at his
toes sanded his history

to dust wrote glass out
of rooftops bones out of
phone lines my father

passed his passport to
the next immigration
officer & took a deep

breath into the knife-
scrawl of the future the
lush lobed hope in his

suitcase the story he'd

tell his unborn daughter
whose name he already

knew & as my father
stepped onto the plane
his father turned in

the bedsheets & grinned
wide in his sleep, the
jackal grin of the living

V

Ars Poetica V: I Want to Know What the World Knows

after Richard Siken

& I can't tell if that's because I'm a poet
or because I have hands. Once, in a dream,
the blank page disappeared & I was finally

content. Obviously, I was supposed to
breathe somehow. That's why I woke up.
Are you daughter, says the page, or are

you artist? To what tense do you pledge
your history? In this world, everything—
well—most things have to do with touch.

Every regret, no exceptions, can be traced
back to the lack of music. So yes, I have
hands. Do I think that makes me taller

than death? All these shimmering tenses
I might steal for my own—I'll leave them
to dry, even if just to prove a point. I'll

exile my hope. I'll say to the world, here
are my hands, right here, where you can
see them. Can I go home now? As if I

need to ask to know the answer. As if
I have time to crunch the numbers,
varnish kills into kindnesses, before

each one becomes weather in my memory.
I say it to the page: look, I didn't ask to
be here. I wanted the world & all I got

was this body, reflected in ink, stationed
close as possible to the nearest exit. Oh
well. We all have to start somewhere.

But I am full of corporeal innocence:
unlike most poets, I know who my
enemies are without needing to bleed

to death for them. Right now I'm treading
mercy like water. My hands are so still
I can call them anything I want. What

the hell could I do with that kind of
power. If whiteness is its own violence
then this must be a crime scene, &

my god, it's worth everything. I see it
now, in the voice of what once called me
faithful, a tense worth stealing from

forever ago: the most beautiful poem
is the absence of mothers who forget.
Everything else is just space on the page.

Seventeen
for Gaia

Someone said *make yourselves useful*
so we made ourselves violent. It was
the year we grew backwards out
of the mouth of our youth, year
seventeen, when there was so much
more we missed than what we'd left
behind. That year we dreamed
the dreams you dream at seventeen,
none of them clean laundry yet
but secrets, daggers, salt on our lips.
We could've loved ourselves but
instead we decided to kill ourselves,
mostly because it seemed like less
work & our packing lists were so long
already. We didn't pray but we drank
our coffee out of the same mugs
every morning, which we decided
was almost the same thing. Besides,
weren't our bodies the least urgent
parts of us? We were seventeen.
We'd seen little enough blood to still
think it terribly romantic. You were
there at the gate, which comes from
the word mouth. Couldn't even look
me in the eye when my flight number
was called—*come on*, I said. *I'm in
love with you, I'm not just killing
time*. But what was love except for
hunger on that seventeenth year,
when I'd never been anything other
than mature for my age? You found
yourself a meaning & pocketed it

like a false passport. We were
seventeen & we knew all our city's
hiding spots, knew all the ways
to wake the water in the air, knew
everything except how to love this
place where we began. One time
I was seventeen & I could see
the things I'd destroyed, with my
hands, could see the echo of them,
shiftless. One time I was seventeen
& I knew every hiding spot in my
city, knew how to imagine all
its unimaginable parts. Years &
taxes later we would run into each
other again in that same airport
terminal & you would look me up
& down & say *wow. You really did
change your life didn't you.* I
was so far from everything I
wanted to be the moment I finally
made up my mind to get better.

In Your Absence

i became an ever rotten thing   i ate my extinction
          & woke to your anatomy   father before i left you
called me wound   now i go by new aliases
          poet   piano chord   strained & caught between
two pillars of light   you raised me a sister of memory
but i   am forgetful still   you raised me
          invention   scared without skin but when she
touches me   i am no longer republic of zero
          no longer   calamity of daughter   in your
absence i am bitter even after absolution   in your
absence i circle back to where you started
          pretending it's the same thing as never having left so
          tell me   how you heard my heartbeat before it
began   & i will tell you how i am you   but crueler
          you in the dialect of her skin you
          transcendent & lonely   you taught me to be good
but in your absence   i think i could settle for happy   with
her it doesn't keep me awake at night   with her i am
          no longer my worst mistake   when she laughs
          i forget how to attack   it's late january
          & the sirens haven't started   but in your
absence i am learning to bless the accidents too
          father teach me   again   to walk into the
flames   teach me again what's golden   when she
touches me i forget how to count   the days until
gravestone   i think if i am   somewhere
i must be home   even half the world away i feel your gaze
          rebuilt   from grief into honey   the
days unspooling into rainfall & the years   like a sky
not stolen but borrowed   in your absence   i
became an ever tragic thing   but when she looks at me i
don't   want to jump anymore   father it's late
january   i know you're still at work   let me pick

you up afterwards   flee the sirens   come home
    & meet the kindest thing   i never was   her
name is girl   i've been everywhere with her
    except for danger

On the First Day of Planting, My Grandmother Becomes Her Garden

She insists that I am a zinnia-whisperer,
which is perhaps the kindest way of

saying this is the only plant in her garden
that I have yet to kill. She gives me the

rake—*how is your heart, kannamma*—
& maybe I will never know another love

as big as her wrists caked in potting soil,
holding each weed she pulls as though it

is the best secret she has ever heard. I say,
I mostly like my classes this semester but

one of my professors is crazy. Dirt falls
through the rake. She digs two fingers into

the soil. When I was younger she would
say to me, *kannamma, some messes are*

worth making. Now she sprinkles fertiliser
into the trench & says, *okay. But how is*

your heart? A goldfinch swoops by: a
promise already kept. I say, *I'm applying*

*for another internship, just for extra pocket
money.* She says, *ask your father for help*

*on your cover letter, it will make him feel
included.* I remember her singing to me

as a child, remember that when I stopped
playing the piano she was the only one in

my family who never asked why. *So how
is your heart?* she says, & pours marigold

seeds into the palm of my hand, lemon
balm in her own. I say, *I've been running*

*more, now that it's warmer. Last week I
beat my personal record.* She says, *good*

for you. & what about your heart? A
cardinal perches on the mailbox. She

covers her seeds in soil, then raises
a watering can & baptises the ground.

Her national flower is spring. I say,
I want to try making your rasmalai

recipe, & she puts down the watering
can, looks me in the eye. The sun is up

& I feel cold anyway. Dahlia seeds
in the soil, catnip & tomatoes, a bird

somewhere I can't see, belting its cares
away. *Kannamma,* she says. *Your heart.*

& I look at her right back. *Grandma,* I
say, *my heart hurts so much. My heart is*

so, so scared. There's something there
about spaciousness, DNA, something

there about what could be instead of
what is, something about how *gold* &

ghost might be the same word if looked
at from afar. When she rises with dirt-

stained knees I think she's going to hug
me but instead, *come inside, kannamma,*

she says. *We forgot the zinnia seeds &*
you know they'll only bloom for you.

In a Dream You Saw a Way to Survive

after Jenny Holzer

in the beginning there was trauma / meaning
girl / first-born child / meaning body
unconquerable // what is a country without
its gods (what is a country without its
women) // meaning / we swim despite the
possibility of drowning / we love / despite
the possibility of living // maybe my country
suffers the same selective amnesia / where
it remembers everything except its own
brutality // there must be a (t)reason for /
all this casual resurrection / the room i live
in claiming my passport / my girlhood for
dust / i inherit causes not symptoms / like
a house not broken into // in this country
there is a story they make out / of tumours /
maybe you've heard of it // it begins with
death it ends / with day & in the middle /
is every other part of the body // repeating
its own name back to itself

VI

Ars Poetica VI: I Promise I Have Better Things to Say Than This

for Natalie

but we can start with the poetry. *I love you like
a midsummer night.* Okay.

I'm tired of making conversation. Logic
is so boring. Let's pour another glass of wine.

Let the mind stain into vapour. Every secret is the
same secret. How about: *I love you in the way good
people kill spiders who do them no harm.* Better.

Once, a friend showed me a tarot card with a fish
jumping out of a young man's cup. Back into the sea.
In most decks, she said, *the fish is still in the cup.*

How about: *I love you in the way this was once a
story about fullness, & now it is a story about loss.*

No. Another glass of wine. Above: the sky
past midnight, its astonishment & ventricles.

I think about the young man, someone's son,
fishless & hungry, the fact of him void of any
shadow. Even so

I think this story is not about a young man
& the things he's lost. I think it is about a fish,

someone's daughter, & the choices she's made.
The sea, someone's mother, & the way she takes
the unrecognisable & gives it form.

How about: *I love you in the way some things will never forget what is theirs.*

It's poetry. Who cares if it makes sense. Before we both woke up you said to me: *I swear I am the young man. Not the fish. Not the sea. Not the empty cup.*

I swear to you I am human. Believe me. Please.
& I did. & I do.

Redemption Theory

when it's over you can choose from the ruin   one name
            to bring back with you   so make it
my name   let my *i* belong to you   my sinew
            unwound by your wishing   my home
brutal & brutalised   cloaked without
fathomable shape   when the soldiers lock you up
        let my breath free your scream   my
superstition the nails in your boots   the canvas on your
skin   your son my father   my neck bared to your
spine   the blood clawing up your throat   always has
a hometown in my mouth   when your language
chokes on foreign tongues   i will kiss it back to life
            i   your saliva pooled in the dark   i
your terror   your terrify   i survive you in your
secrets   i do all this & more for the moon swallowing
            your memory's skin i shrivel   into
the only hope smaller than thunder   into the space
between you & you again   your palms my psalms
        my bones brittle   as the wind that raised you
            the birds busy pasting my eyelids shut
        so you don't have to watch the death   of your
heritage   all split veins   writing through to home
            all culture   severed in two   the
maps with their ears their agonies   their hard-earned
lies   some things   are better left
imagined   but i think this country could be mine if i
knew how to pronounce it   by which i mean
        i think it could be yours

No Accident

My favourite poet is change.

There was a hurricane before I was born,
I think, or maybe it was just my grandmother
calling me to earth. No matter.

Name it myth for now. Teach your grandmother
how to use the voice memos on her phone.
Don't write it down yet. Just listen.

I had a history once but
I traded it for New Jersey's only good roti prata.

A tearing sound & sudden rain. Name it myth.
I loved this language once, before
I knew any better.

So I failed the test, chose
my people instead. I was full of good prata,
mango pickle. It was late, in this time zone.

I think there was a hurricane but maybe it was
just my friends, telling me to hurry up

& get in the car before the food gets cold.
I've been jetlagged from birth, mistaken
into orbit, loved on both sides of the Atlantic.

Car windows rolled down, three languages
on the radio. We're foreign enough tonight

that nothing could possibly stop us,
American enough that nothing dares to try.

That's how you know you're home—
in the background of your grandmother's voice
memo, you know every raindrop by its name.

Someone standing
in the street behind you yells *despair*
& you're too busy laughing

to even turn around.

2 A.M., the Eve of New Year's Eve

My parents are arguing
over whether to buy a new

piano. My father says
let's take a deep breath &

think about this rationally.
My mother squalls out of

the room, into mine. She says
it's impossible to do this with him.

*He doesn't understand
how a body thirsts for music.*

Years away in Philadelphia
the music in my earphones

stops at 2 A.M. The next
morning, New Year's Eve,

I wake up & learn that my father
has had his first epileptic seizure.

My father is a mathematician.
He dislikes the music

that made me. Even so
when I was a child he would

dance across the kitchen floor
with my feet on his. Tell me

sweetheart, you are my
favourite song's favourite song.

Years away in Singapore
my lover asks about my

father & I say *he is the best*
person I know, & I hope never

to be like him. My philosophy
professor says *the thing*

Plato called math, Cicero
called music, the way my father

knew my name for 20 years
before I was born but

to this day must still be
reminded of my birthday.

Years away my childhood
home is cluttered with too many

instruments. The piano in our
entryway is older than I am.

I call my father at 2 A.M.,
his time, & he always picks up.

I am every sickness
he can't leave behind.

I am every differential he
has dreamed into song.

My mother says *some people*
can be musicians all their lives

& never once realise it. Tonight,
years away in Philadelphia,

the calendar has just turned
December 31st. The past

hushed in wait for morning
& her rituals of newness.

Against the window my future
selves knock, but I've

already restarted the playlist.
I readjust my earphones. I skip

the song called forgiveness,
then I go back & play it again.

Notes on Arrival

That night you opened your mouth to say it
& only dust came out. So you improvised.
Instead of saying it, you coughed & out
came pennies. Instead of opening your
mouth you opened the window to let
the rain in. The bed was already packed
so you slept on the floor, even though it
was damp. You made a home out of the
chests of minor gods & when you inhaled
you tasted envy. The world was ablaze so
you opened your good wine without
any occasion. You missed your plane &
you adored all the noise. Everyone in your
introductory calculus class wanted you
to be safe. You caught a cold but you did
not apologise. Your father kept calling but
you did not apologise. You lied yourself
awake. When your lover opened your door
all he found inside were cardboard boxes.
You undressed electricity out of its copper.
You counted backwards from 10,000
because your psychiatrist said it might help.
You only got to 5,000 but it didn't help.
So you improvised. You learned a fourth
language, a new number system, & you
counted the rest of the way down. You
bought a new plane ticket. You finished
your good wine & you bought new wine.
You baked bread. You practised every city
you'd ever left. When you told him *I'm
in love with someone else* he didn't stop
texting you & when you told him *please
stop texting me* he didn't stop texting you.

So you improvised. You blocked his
number. You found a guitar on a sidewalk
& you took it home. You apologised
for the first time in years & for the first
time in years you received forgiveness.
You bought pink hair dye & you put it in
your carry-on. You threw the cardboard
boxes out the window. When you finally
walked off the plane it was 22 years late
& you were bowed beneath the weight
of all you'd survived. Your father on
the tarmac barely recognised you but
still he looked that stranger in the eye.
He welcomed her as if the emergency
were over, as if home were a nickname
for the first day of both their lives.

Acknowledgements

A million times thank you—

To Blythe Baird, for your boundless generosity & care with my work, & for the rose petals, & for the boxed wine.

To Tanesha Nicole Tyler & Sam Van Cook, who said yes, who keep saying yes.

To Tanvi Dutta Gupta & Danie Shokoohi, who have been here from the start.

To monsoon season. To home.

To those whose light keeps me here: Camille Reeves, Sam Spector, Ashlee Culmsee, Kagiso Lesego Molope, Maisie McPherson, Caitlin Conlon, Jeremy Bernius, Lyd Havens, Kate Wilson, Lucy Hannah Ryan, AG McGee, Rooya Rahin, Kendrick Loo, Ollie van den Heuvel, Jocelyn Suarez, Cyril Wong, Cissy Li, Dmitry Kharchenko, Gwyneth Teo, Zara Williams, Chu Jia Sing, Brittani Telfair, Stephanie Tom, Paola Bennet, Hana Widerman, Juan Hermo, & Gaia Rajan.

To all the late nights at Alchemy Bistro & all the early mornings at Small World Coffee.

To Songline Slam & the Atom Collective, who saw most of these poems in their earliest forms.

To the readers, of course & always.

To my father, who gave me his courage & his eyes, & from whom I am learning every day. To my family, to whom I owe everything.

I am so lucky & so proud to love you. "Grateful" doesn't even cover it.

Notes

"Ars Poetica V: I Want to Know What the World Knows" is loosely based on Richard Siken's poem "The Way the Light Reflects".

"In a Dream You Saw a Way to Survive" takes its title from Jenny Holzer's *Truisms* series.

"Departure Time", "Every Day the Same Story About Immigrants", "I Found a New World Across the Sea", & "Ars Poetica III: This Must Be the Place" were previously published in the 2020 Singapore Writers Festival Installation *Letters From Home to Home*.

"Every Day the Same Story About Immigrants" was previously published in the August 2019 issue of *Ghost City Review*.

"I Found a New World Across the Sea" was previously published in Issue 8 of *Under a Warm Green Linden*.

"So, Stranger" was previously published in *EXHALE: An Anthology of Queer Singapore Voices* (Math Paper Press, 2021).

"War Story With My Father" was previously published in Issue 14 of *Sundog Lit* & recognised by the 2018 Ellis Awards.

"Ars Poetica II: Season Finale of the American Dream" was previously published in Issue 43 of *The Moth*.

"Birkshire Lane" was previously published in Issue 11 of *Occulum*.

"That Summer I Wrote the Same Poem Over & Over" & "Notes on Arrival" were previously published in Volume 14, Number 1 of *diode*.

"Ars Poetica VI: I Promise I Have Better Things to Say Than This" was previously recognised by the 2019 Singapore National Poetry Competition.

Bio

Topaz Winters is the author of the full-length poetry collections *Portrait of My Body as a Crime I'm Still Committing* (2019) & *poems for the sound of the sky before thunder* (2017), & of the chapbook *Heaven or This* (2016). She is the founder & editor-in-chief of the publishing house & literary journal Half Mystic. Her peer-reviewed research on poetry, identity, & queerness in Singapore is published in the *Journal of Homosexuality.* Her creative work has been published in *Sundog Lit, diode,* & *Tinderbox Poetry Journal;* profiled by *The Straits Times, The Business Times,* & *Entropy;* & featured at the Boston Poetry Slam, the Singapore Writers Festival, & the Other Tongues Literary Festival. Topaz studies English, Visual Art, & Italian at Princeton University. She is 22 years old, & likes bees, baklava, & bookstores.

OTHER BOOKS BY BUTTON POETRY

If you enjoyed this book, please consider checking out some of our others, below. Readers like you allow us to keep broadcasting and publishing. Thank you!

Neil Hilborn, *Our Numbered Days*

Hanif Abdurraqib, *The Crown Ain't Worth Much*

Sabrina Benaim, *Depression & Other Magic Tricks*

Rudy Francisco, *Helium*

Rachel Wiley, *Nothing Is Okay*

Neil Hilborn, *The Future*

Phil Kaye, *Date & Time*

Andrea Gibson, *Lord of the Butterflies*

Blythe Baird, *If My Body Could Speak*

Desireé Dallagiacomo, *SINK*

Dave Harris, *Patricide*

Michael Lee, *The Only Worlds We Know*

Raych Jackson, *Even the Saints Audition*

Brenna Twohy, *Swallowtail*

Porsha Olayiwola, *i shimmer sometimes, too*

Jared Singer, *Forgive Yourself These Tiny Acts of Self-Destruction*

Adam Falkner, *The Willies*

George Abraham, *Birthright*

Omar Holmon, *We Were All Someone Else Yesterday*

Rachel Wiley, *Fat Girl Finishing School*

Bianca Phipps, *crown noble*

Rudy Francisco, *I'll Fly Away*

Natasha T. Miller, *Butcher*

Kevin Kantor, *Please Come Off-Book*

Ollie Schminkey, *Dead Dad Jokes*

Reagan Myers, *Afterwards*

L.E. Bowman, *What I Learned From the Trees*

Patrick Roche, *A Socially Acceptable Breakdown*

Andrea Gibson, *You Better Be Lightning*

Rachel Wiley, *Revenge Body*

Ebony Stewart, *BloodFresh*

Ebony Stewart, *Home.Girl.Hood.*

Kyle Tran Mhyre, *Not A Lot of Reasons to Sing, but Enough*

Steven Willis, *A Peculiar People*

Available at buttonpoetry.com/shop and more!